essential careers™

A CAREER AS A
CHEF

SUSAN MEYER

ROSEN
PUBLISHING
NEW YORK

Published in 2013 by The Rosen Publishing Group, Inc.
29 East 21st Street, New York, NY 10010

First Edition

Library of Congress Cataloging-in-Publication Data

Meyer, Susan, 1986–
 A career as a chef/Susan Meyer.
     p. cm.—(Essential careers)
Includes bibliographical references and index.
ISBN 978-1-4488-8236-6 (library binding)
1. Cooking—Vocational guidance—Juvenile literature. I. Title.
TX652.4.M49 2013
641.50023—dc23

                                                    2012020143

Manufactured in the United States of America

CPSIA Compliance Information: Batch #W13YA: For further information, contact Rosen Publishing, New York, New York, at 1-800-237-9932.

contents

INTRO

Becoming a chef is a very rewarding career choice. However, it takes a lot of hard work and planning to become successful in the food industry.

DUCTION

From the sights and smells of standing in front of a grill and achieving a perfect medium rare steak to the methodical joy of employing expert knife skills in cutting potatoes into precise matchstick fries, the life of a chef can be a wonderful career for those who truly love the preparation of food. If you are someone who never gets tired of cooking and discovering new foods to prepare and new methods of preparation, you just might have what it takes to be a chef.

In trying economic times, training to be a chef can be a relatively safe choice. There are some careers that seem to do well despite the ups and downs of the economy. These careers are in industries that provide an essential service that people just can't do without. The food service and restaurant industry has a number of these careers because, no matter what, people have to eat. Of course, it's true that people don't always have to eat the best, and they could probably survive on foods that they scrounged up and prepared on their own. However, research shows that even in economic downturns people can't help but enjoy themselves by eating out. Who doesn't love kicking back and letting someone else cook after a long day? Very few people, as it turns out.

In fact, so many people in the United States eat out each year that the total annual sales of food and drink at restaurants are estimated to be over $6 billion! Clearly, American diners are hungry, but what is more interesting is that this number sharply increased from around $4 billion dollars in the year 2000. People are hungry for a chef's creations, and the economic

Research shows that even during recent periods of economic recession, families still enjoy going out to eat and letting a professional take over their meal preparation.

downturn of the last few years hasn't dampened that hunger. The number of restaurants has increased dramatically in the last fifty years. In the last five years, there has been an explosion of chain restaurants that provide convenient, reliable food for the average family. An increase in the number of restaurants means an increase in the number of jobs in restaurants—jobs that will be filled by the enterprising chefs of tomorrow.

What follows can be used as a tool to understanding what it takes to be a chef and fill this essential position. Some of the characteristics of a working chef, what the job is like day-to-day, and the many difficult steps one must take in order to have a successful career in the culinary industry will be explained. Additionally, the different types of chefs and the different places they work—both in restaurants and in other, more unexpected venues—will be delved into. Also examined will be the way the culinary and food service industry is changing as more and more people begin to care about what is in their food and where the ingredients they eat come from. First and foremost, the goal is for you to get a definite sense of whether or not this intense, but rewarding, career path is a good fit for you.

chapter 1

WHAT IT TAKES TO BE A CHEF

For most young and aspiring chefs, their first interest in cooking and preparing food started right in their home kitchen. Many well-known chefs today recall their earliest food memories as learning to cook with a parent or grandparent or trying out new flavors and flavor combinations to produce things for their very first customers: themselves and their family members.

Today's would-be chefs might be encouraged by the images of celebrity chefs they see on television. The chef's profession is getting much more acclaim and media attention than ever before. You might have seen chefs on television shows who get to meet celebrities and travel the world, all because of their talent in the kitchen. However, it's important to realize that these experiences are not the norm.

It's also important to know that cooking professionally as a chef is a very demanding career choice. It can be incredibly rewarding for the right person, but make no bones about it: it's a lot of hard work. The hours are long, and work is frequently required on nights, weekends, and holidays. While other people are off work and enjoying nice evenings out at restaurants, chefs are the ones helping to make sure they enjoy their leisure time with some delicious food. The job is also physically demanding. As for the working conditions, they are—as you might imagine—hot.

Aspiring chefs must have a passion for and sincerely love food preparation and cooking in its humblest form.

One of the best places for an aspiring chef to start out is in his or her home kitchen. Cooking with your family will also help you learn more about your cultural food heritage.

THE INGREDIENTS REQUIRED FOR A SUCCESSFUL CHEF

There are a number of qualities that anyone who wants to be a chef should have. You must be creative and have a passion for food. Most people who set their sights on this career do it out of a love for creating new and unique flavor combinations in food. You must also have a willingness to learn—either in a culinary school or training program or on the job in a kitchen. There are an incredible number of skills that a chef has to learn, and the only way to develop these skills and techniques is to practice. A lot of learning to be a chef is simply doing something so many times that it becomes second nature.

Knife skills, for example, are an important part of being a chef. If you've ever seen professional chefs chopping vegetables, you can't help but be impressed by how quickly their hands move and how the pieces they chop are somehow

With a number of critically acclaimed restaurants and well known television shows, Gordon Ramsey is one of the rare chefs who is well-known outside the industry.

perfectly uniform despite the great knife speed. This skill comes from hours and hours of practice (and more than a few bandages in the early stages).

Another important quality of any aspiring chef is to simply enjoy the act of food preparation in and of itself, as its own end rather than a means to an end. If you're hoping to achieve fame and fortune, you probably should not enter the culinary industry. Very few chefs in the industry get their own show on television or open restaurants in big cities all over the world. For every Emeril Lagasse, Anthony Bourdain, Rachael Ray, or Gordon Ramsay, there are many hundreds of men and women working anonymously all over the country in the kitchens of greasy spoon diners, big name chain eateries, mall food courts, and hotel restaurants. A good chef appreciates food prepara-tion and enjoys providing an essential service to people regard-less of where he or she does it.

A good chef must also be creative. This, in part, means that the chef can think outside the box and make new, unique food combinations. To stand out in the culinary industry, chefs need to be able to think of ways to set their food apart from others and really forge an identity for themselves. A good chef must also be able to work well on a team. The head chef must be good at delegating responsibilities to the other chefs in the kitchen. The lower chefs must be able to take orders well and carry them out efficiently. Working as a chef is definitely not a good career path for someone who likes to work and succeed by him- or herself. The successes or failures of a kitchen on any given night depend upon the whole team.

A chef must work well under pressure. The atmosphere in a kitchen can range from a tense calm to a frenzied excitement. A chef cannot be fazed by people yelling orders, tight deadlines, and kitchen mishaps. Every second a chef spends in a kitchen involves a tight deadline. Only a few seconds separate an item that is undercooked from one that is just right or from one that is burned. A good chef is always on his or her toes and displays enormous grace under pressure.

Beyond all the strong mental qualities a chef must possess, there are some important physical ones, too. Training to be a chef can be like boot camp. Chefs are on their feet all night, and not just standing still. They are running back and forth from various burners to counters to the pantry to get more ingredients. There is also the enormous arm strength required to carry out tasks like chopping 40 pounds (18 kilograms) of potatoes or whisking egg whites into a meringue or deboning twelve ducks. Working in a kitchen isn't always a picnic, and it requires a lot of mental and physical strength, but to those who can take the heat, it can also be a lot of fun.

THE BUSINESS OF BEING A CHEF

Having a good business sense is a quality that is sometimes overlooked but one that chefs really need to be successful. This

A good chef must be able to handle multiple tasks—and sometimes multiple foods—all at the same time. It's a job that requires you to be both quick on your feet and good with your hands.

is particularly true if one of your goals in becoming a chef is to own your own restaurant—whether it is a place of your own design or a franchise of a larger chain restaurant. However, even if you don't aspire to own a restaurant and are happy operating

For chefs who own their restaurants, there is far more to being a chef than just food preparation. They must deal with suppliers, government inspections, insurance adjusters, budgets, and much more.

someone else's kitchen, it's still important to understand how and why a restaurant makes money. It's even more important to understand how and why a restaurant loses money.

A restaurant is, first and foremost, a type of business.

The only way the business stays open is if it makes enough money to cover all its expenses, ideally with a healthy profit left over. In addition to knowing how to cook, a chef who wants to own a restaurant also must have financial and managerial skills. Just as you can go to school to learn how to cook and prepare food, you can also take classes in learning to run a small business. It is easy to educate yourself on how to run a restaurant, as long as you realize the magnitude of the undertaking.

Most new restaurants fail within a year of opening, and every year many long-established restaurants close. Restaurants fail for a number of different reasons. Many of these reasons have nothing to do with the quality of the food. While the food is the most important part of any restaurant, it is not the only part. A chef can make the best menu in the world and the restaurant can still fail if he or she doesn't take into account a multitude of other variables.

The restaurant must have a good location where it is highly visible and people will be able to get to it easily. A good staff must be assembled and maintained. Waitstaff, hosts, and other front of the house positions must be filled, as well as all of the assistant chef positions in the kitchen. The front of the house positions are just as important as those in the kitchen because these people will interact with customers in a way that the chef and cooks can't. The restaurant-owning chef also has to consider the ambience of the restaurant. The overall feel of the restaurant should be inviting and should complement the food that the restaurant serves. You wouldn't want to order a $40 filet mignon in a place with sticky floors and

WHAT A CHEF WEARS

When you think of a chef, you might picture a person in a stiff white jacket, possibly wearing an apron. Undoubtedly you imagine the one thing that has become an icon of the culinary industry—the tall, white hat. This hat is called a toque. Wearing a hat in the kitchen is an important part of any chef's uniform because it is part of following health code guidelines. It keeps the chef's hair from getting in the food.

Today the standard uniform of a chef is anything but standard or uniform. Most kitchens today require chefs to wear a double-breasted jacket that will prevent them from getting harmed by spills and the heat of stoves. The traditional chef's pants are a black-and-white checkered pattern, although, depending on the kitchen, many chefs have a lot more freedom in choosing their leg wear and can wear pants of a variety of different patterns and fabrics. Mostly chefs just need something that will hold up to multiple washings and allow them the freedom to move.

plastic furniture. The look of the restaurant goes a long way to selling the food before it even gets to the plate.

DAILY LIFE IN A KITCHEN

The day-to-day work in a kitchen is physically grueling. Chefs deal with heavy pans and ingredients—from bags of flour to sacks of potatoes—and are on their feet for long periods of time. In addition to gaining big muscles, new chefs must also learn to grow a thick skin. They must have a strong and confident personality and learn to take criticism well. In the high-pressure environment of a professional kitchen, even the smallest mistakes are often met with harsh feedback. This isn't true of all kitchens, of course, but for those who don't take constructive criticism well, becoming a chef is not a great career choice. New chefs will make a lot of mistakes before they learn how to do everything right, and while they're learning they have to put up with a lot of critical feedback—sometimes being shouted at them at top volume.

A DAY IN THE LIFE OF A HEAD CHEF

A chef's day is very long—especially for a head chef and even more for one who has an ownership stake in the business. A chef at an average-sized restaurant might arrive at nine or ten in the morning to make sure the necessary produce, meats, and other foods were delivered overnight. If there are problems, the chef might have to call the restaurant's suppliers to complain.

Mid-morning, the chef might start preparing (or supervising the preparation of) sauces and desserts or any food items that require a long time to cook or prepare. Around 11:30, the restaurant will open for lunch and the chef will need to start cranking out dishes for the busy lunch rush, which usually lasts until 2:00. From 2:00 until 4:00, the head chef might have time to review stocks and see what the kitchen needs to order. At 4:00, he or she can go over the specials for the evening with the sous-chefs and the waitstaff.

Depending on the restaurant, the dinner rush can last anywhere from 6:00 to 10:00 or 11:00 at night. After the last meal is served and the last customer is seen happily out the door, the chef can supervise what needs to be done for the next day. Only then can he or she head before home around midnight or later to get a few hours of sleep and begin the whole process again the next morning.

chapter 2

MANY KITCHENS, MANY CHEFS

There are a number of qualities and skills a successful chef must possess. While it's true that most skilled chefs have these things in common, it's important to note that not all chef jobs are created equal. There are a wealth of different options available in the culinary industry. Learning more about these career choices can help you focus on which opportunities best suit your individual goals and interests.

As previously mentioned, a very small number of people become the kind of celebrity chef who makes lots of money and appears on television. There are a far greater number of equally talented and passionate chefs and food preparation workers who don't get the same public acclaim and glory, but who do what they do simply because they enjoy making good food. We will look at all the different kinds of chefs and all the places you might find them—from restaurants, cruise ships, and hotels to private homes and even grocery stores.

WHERE TO FIND A CHEF

The classic image of a chef is a commanding figure hard at work leading a troop of sous-chefs in the enormous commercial kitchen of a restaurant. However, chefs can be found working in many other places in addition to restaurants.

Being a chef doesn't mean that you have to be stuck in a sweltering indoor kitchen or even confined to land! Here, chefs are grilling at an outdoor café for diners on a cruise ship.

Basically, almost anywhere you find prepared food, there is a chef working hard behind the scenes.

Chefs work in hotels and on cruise ships preparing food for the guests. A hotel offers a great variety of opportunities for a chef. Hotel kitchens are often very structured and very large because they are serving hundreds if not thousands of guests. When working in a hotel kitchen, a chef is not just preparing breakfast, lunch, and dinner, but also buffets, brunches, and room service, and catering for weddings, conferences, and other special events.

Chefs who specialize in off-site catering experience their own unique challenges. They might never know what the kitchen they will be working in will be like until they get there. They have to travel with all of their tools. And most difficult of all, they have to serve a huge number of people all at once.

The food served in school cafeterias has improved greatly in recent years, as new emphasis has been placed on healthy options and fresh, quality ingredients. Cafeteria cooks work not only in schools, but also in colleges, office buildings, nursing homes, and hospitals all over the country. They have the difficult job of making mass amounts of food for a huge group of people. And this food should be characterized not just by its quantity, but also by its quality. Cafeteria chefs may also have to follow stricter health and nutrition guidelines that will alter how their food will taste.

Another place it's easy for chefs to go unnoticed is in grocery stores. While most people who are grocery shopping focus on all of the food that they have to go home and cook themselves, think about some of the food in the store that's already made. If the grocery store has a salad bar, that means a prep cook had to chop and prepare all those vegetables, lettuces, and salads. If the deli counter has prepared pasta salads or pre-seasoned meats, a chef had to make those, too. And what grocery store would be complete without a bakery? A chef made those breads and desserts that are so hard to resist.

It's easy to remember that chefs are responsible for your delicious meal in a restaurant, but even in other venues they are often responsible for the food you love. Pastry chefs work tirelessly to make the rolls at your local bakery and grocery, for example.

Some chefs don't prepare food for large crowds of people at restaurants or hotels, but instead cook for a small number of people. Personal chefs usually work in their employers' homes. They are completely in charge of the preparation of meals, usually even including choosing and buying the ingredients. They must plan a menu based on the preferences, dietary restrictions, and allergies of the family for whom they cook. This type of job can allow a personal chef greater freedom and more time off than that enjoyed by his or her restaurant colleagues.

CHEFS UP AND DOWN THE LINE

You will notice that a lot of the names for different positions in the culinary arts derive from the French. This is because a lot of these terms and titles originated in France in the nineteenth century, but today they are used in kitchens all over the world. The word "chef" actually comes from the French *chef de cuisine* which means "chief of the kitchen" in English. Today, the word "chef" has come to mean not just the head of the kitchen, but any culinary professional regardless of his or her rank. The title executive chef or head chef is used to identify the person who is truly the kitchen chief. The executive chef is the ultimate authority in the kitchen. This person decides what should be on the menu and how it should be prepared, right down to how it should appear on the plate. He or she manages the kitchen staff and is also often in charge of the ordering and purchasing of inventory—deciding what foods to buy and whom to buy them from.

Working under the executive chef is the sous-chef. In fact, "sous-chef" literally means "under chief" in French. The sous-chef is the second-in-command in the kitchen. This person is responsible for carrying out the executive chef's orders and instructions. The sous-chef is also responsible for filling in for the executive chef when he or she is off duty. Sometimes the

A big part of a head chef's job is planning the restaurant's menu. When deciding what food to prepare and serve, he or she must consider things like what foods are in season, what dishes sell well, and what is in the restaurant's budget.

head chef is the owner of the restaurant. In these cases, the sous-chef might actually be in charge of running the kitchen, while the head chef is occupied with running the restaurant as a whole. Smaller restaurants may not have a sous-chef, but large restaurants may have more than one—a day sous-chef and a night sous-chef. The sous-chef, as the second most important person in the kitchen, usually gets to handle the most expensive ingredients that some of the lower chefs don't get to work with.

Although the job varies from restaurant to restaurant, a sous-chef's duties may also include ordering supplies, training new staff, and expediting during lunch or dinner service. In the chef world, expediting means helping to pace the meals so that they go out of the kitchen at the right time. It is often a difficult juggling act to make sure the food for each table goes out at the same time and at the optimum temperature.

Below the sous-chef are the chefs de parties, also known as the line cooks or station cooks. Each line cook is in charge of a certain station in the kitchen. Say you go

THE SWEET LIFE OF A PASTRY CHEF

Few people can't appreciate the sweet successes of a good pastry chef. In a typical restaurant, the pastry chef might be in charge of baking bread for the restaurant, as well as preparing the best part of any meal: the dessert. From ice cream and custard to tarts and cakes, these specially trained chefs know their way around sugar and flour.

Being a pastry chef is very different from being a regular line or station cook. The pastry chef typically works independently of the other chefs. This chef often starts the day very early and finishes his or her work by the lunch rush. It is also a different type of culinary work involving a number of unique and specialized skills and cooking and baking techniques. What makes most cooking both fun and challenging is that the chef must use a degree of instinct to season something just right. He or she can be improvisational and mix and measure ingredients "on the fly" and to taste. With baking and dessert making, however, the chef needs to demonstrate an attention to detail and concern for proper math and precise measurements. If the butter is not the proper temperature or the precise measurement of an ingredient is not added at exactly the right time, the whole dessert could be a disaster.

When it comes to desserts, there are usually two people involved: the pastry chef who produces the dessert and the service person who ultimately puts it on the plate. The service person is in charge of plating the dessert with the appropriate garnish and sauces and making it lovely...just before you devour every last bite.

to a nice restaurant and order a steak that comes with a side of green beans. You also order a salad to start. If it is a large restaurant, your meal may be made by several different cooks. One line cook might man the grill to make sure your steak comes out perfectly, while another might be in charge of cooking vegetables, and yet another might plate your salad. Everyone in a kitchen has to work as a team to make sure every customer's order is prepared correctly and sent out at just the right temperature and the right time.

There are even more kinds of chefs under the umbrella of station cooks because the chef who works at each station has a different title. The man or woman who cooked your steak? That's the grill chef. The creator of your green beans was likely the sauté chef (sometimes known by the French word *saucier*) who is in charge of all sautéed items and their sauces. The culinary professional who plated your salad? He or she is known as the garde-manger. The garde-manger is in charge of preparing cold items from salads to cold appetizers. The garde-manger is often considered a starting position in the kitchen because there is less training required to prepare some of these foods. Nevertheless, the garde-manger is a vitally important part of the kitchen staff. After all, the foods from the garde-manger's station are often responsible for the diners' first impressions of the meal.

There is an equally important person who handles the meal's final impression. If you still have any room left after your steak and you choose to order a dessert, it would be prepared by the pastry chef.

Below the station cook is the commis. The commis is an assistant or apprentice to the station cook. This is an entry-level position. The commis is able to learn valuable skills from the cook under whom he or she is working. He or she can gain valuable knife and food preparation skills while experiencing the fast pace and pressures of a real kitchen environment.

Not all chefs slave over a hot stove. Some, such as this garde-manger, have the important tasks of preparing perfect salads and other cold items.

Similar to the commis, but not always thought of as an apprentice position, is the prep cook. In many ways the prep cook is the backbone of the kitchen. He or she does a lot of the more basic, humble, physically grueling but essential tasks, like chopping all the vegetables for the night or mincing all the garlic. The prep cook might even butcher some of the less expensive cuts of meat so that they will be ready when the more experienced chefs are ready to use them.

All of these positions are very important in the kitchen— be it in a fashionable city restaurant, in a suburban chain eatery, on a cruise ship, or in someone's private home. In order to join the kitchen hierarchy, a chef must learn the basic skills necessary. Additionally, chefs must refine their palettes and learn new flavors and combinations to which they haven't yet been exposed.

chapter 3

LEARNING THE TRICKS OF THE TRADE

The journey to becoming a chef is all about choices. One of the first choices you have to make is whether you will go to culinary school or not. Not every chef has gone to culinary school. Many successful chefs have risen to the top of their profession by starting at the bottom, as line and prep cooks and even dishwashers. They worked their way up without any formal education in culinary arts. Many of the skills you need to become a whiz with a knife or whip up perfect sauces can be learned right in the kitchen at whatever restaurant hires you.

Establishing one's career as a chef by first attending culinary arts school has some definite advantages. The formal training you will receive, sometimes from highly regarded industry professionals, can be invaluable, as can the opportunity to be exposed to a wide range of kitchen settings, cooking styles and techniques, and culinary traditions and tastes. Of course, there are some drawbacks to a culinary arts education, too. And if you do decide the pros outweigh the cons, you still have to decide which of the vast array of schools to attend.

Is Culinary School the Right Choice?

If you wanted to be a biologist, you would most certainly have to go to school to study in a classroom, do research in the library and labs, and participate in field projects to gain the body of knowledge and practical skills necessary for a career in the field. But is the same true of cooking? In culinary school, you will learn some of the history and methods behind culinary arts, but most of what you will be doing is hands-on experiential learning. Is it better to learn in a classroom setting than in a working kitchen in a real restaurant?

Some of the advantages of culinary school are that you are able to learn new skills in a controlled environment. You can also learn both local and global techniques. If you are working at a restaurant in a small Midwestern town hundreds of miles from the nearest big city, you might not have the same access to the increasingly popular and in-demand techniques of Malaysian cuisine, for example, or South American taste traditions. Formal academic training will give you a much broader range of knowledge, skills, techniques, and culinary references. You will also have hands-on, supportive, personalized help and be working with teachers whose primary goal is to mold you into a better chef.

Another advantage of formal training is that it is often part of a college or university program that allows students to work toward official certification as a chef. Upon graduation, when you are looking for your first job, you will already be recognized as a chef. This might help you start a few rungs up on the ladder. Not only will you possibly be able to start in a higher position in the kitchen, but you might also be eligible for a higher starting salary. Additionally, going to culinary school can help you make valuable connections in the restaurant world. You will get a well-rounded sense of culinary history

In culinary school, young chefs can learn important cooking skills and techniques from experienced chefs in a controlled environment.

and learn a number of different techniques and traditions.

There are some downsides to culinary school, however, and they need to be considered carefully. Although there are shorter (and less prestigious) culinary training programs you can join, most degree-granting programs require two to four years of study in order to earn certification. Additionally, the cost of culinary school is much higher than other methods of training. Unlike receiving your culinary training on the job, you are not getting paid when you attend culinary school. In fact, you are paying—often quite handsomely—to enroll in the classes. When you graduate from culinary school, you will still have to pay your dues in the kitchen. While culinary school might give you the knowledge, techniques, experience, and certification to start a little higher in the kitchen hierarchy and rise a little faster, it still takes a lot of hard work, long hours, and low wages to become a high-ranking chef.

Getting into a top culinary school can be incredibly competitive. There are far more people interested in attending the best schools than there are available places in the programs. You also have to be careful when choosing a school. Not all schools are created equal. Make sure to do your research and learn what sort of credentials the school will offer you and if it is well-known and respected in the culinary world. Try to find information on how many of the program's graduates get placed in culinary jobs soon after graduation and if the school boasts any alumni who have become prominent professionals in the field.

SCHOOLS TO CONSIDER

If you decide that culinary school is the right choice for you, there are still a number of decisions to make. There are several questions you have to ask yourself to help choose a program that will be a good fit. Are you interested in attending—and can you afford—a two- or a four-year program? What is your budget for attending a culinary program? Do you want to go full-time or part-time? During the day or in the evening? What type of cooking are you interested in focusing on or specializing in?

There are a great number of culinary schools out there with

good reputations that you can attend. There is an option to suit any aspiring chef's schedule, budget, and needs. There are four-year degree programs that offer bachelor's degrees and other nondegree courses that offer certificates that might take only a

The Ristorante Caterina de' Medici, shown here, is one of five student-run restaurants at the Culinary Institute of America in Hyde Park, New York. Working at these restaurants enables students to get some real-life, on-the-job culinary experience.

few months. The downside of this great variety of options is that it can be hard to choose just one.

One of the most well-known culinary programs in the United States is the Culinary Institute of American (or, CIA, as it is sometimes called). This four-year university is the oldest culinary school in the United States. It was founded in 1946 in Connecticut. Today, however, it is located in Hyde Park, New York. Over the years, the school has produced over thirty-five thousand new chefs. The CIA is a residential school, meaning students live on campus while learning all about the world of culinary arts.

The CIA is a well-respected program both in the United States and around the world. The CIA offers a well-rounded program that covers everything from American and international cooking techniques to nutrition science and sanitation, as well as hospitality and restaurant management. The goal of the institution is to produce well-rounded chefs ready for their first job in any kitchen. The program also requires students to work in one of four on-campus restaurants and also to complete a one-semester externship. An externship is like an internship, but usually shorter in duration and often set up by an institution. It is a period of time spent working in a restaurant for the purpose of gaining practical experience. An extern-ship, like an internship, can be paid or unpaid.

While the Culinary Institute of America is the oldest culinary school in the country, it is far from the only

Students at the prestigious Johnson & Wales University in Rhode Island learn the importance of speed and efficiency in the kitchen while working at the on-campus deli.

top-notch institution. Johnson & Wales University in Providence, Rhode Island (with other locations in Charleston, South Carolina, and Norfolk, Virginia), is a well-regarded school that offers associate's, bachelor's, and graduate degrees in food service and hospitality. Another leading culinary arts program is the Institute of Culinary Education in New York City, which offers eight- to thirteen-month career training programs in culinary arts, pastry and baking arts, and culinary management. It was founded by Peter Kump, a founding member of the James Beard Foundation, an organization devoted to culinary excellence. On the other side of the country, there is the California Culinary Academy in San Francisco, which runs a sixteen-month program that includes closely monitored apprenticeships. An apprenticeship is a great way for new chefs to gain on-the-job kitchen experience with top chefs.

COOKING FOR THE TROOPS

It is important not to overlook another potential way to gain culinary certification and hands-on professional experience: the U.S. military. The U.S. Military Chef Certification program offers qualified applicants the opportunity to certify their food service skills and knowledge by working in the armed forces as culinary professionals, serving food to those who serve the nation.

The American Culinary Federation (ACF) is the largest organization of professional chefs in North America. The ACF has a certification program with a number of different levels that chefs

Here, two culinary specialists 2nd class at the Naval Amphibious Base Coronado plate their dishes to achieve the perfect presentation in a navy culinary competition.

can reach. Through the U.S. Military Certification program, talented chefs who are serving in the military are taught the skills they need to achieve these important certifications. The certifications are not determined by title or military rank. Instead, they are determined by an applicant's actual culinary knowledge and kitchen skills. The education and hands-on experience chefs can gain by working in military kitchens may qualify them for one or more ACF certification levels, which can help pave the way for civilian culinary careers.

Obviously, this path is not for everyone. But for those who have an interest in working in the military, as well as a passion for food, it is possible to combine the two and end up with both experience and certification—and ultimately a paying job.

Applying to Culinary School

Many of the top culinary programs are extremely competitive and are unable to admit all of the qualified applicants who apply. It is therefore important for potential applicants to learn how to make sure that their applications stand out from the pack.

The CIA requires high school transcripts, letters of recommendation, an essay explaining why the applicant wishes to study culinary arts, and a résumé with the applicant's background in the food service industry. Not all culinary schools ask for a background in the food service industry as a prerequisite for application. The CIA, however, requires a minimum of three to five months of food service experience, at least some of which must have been in a professional kitchen.

Make sure to do your research when looking for the culinary school that is the perfect fit for you. Visit their Web sites and read any brochures and literature they have available. Look at their courses and see if they cover a range of techniques and skills, particularly those that you are most interested in learning. It is also important to consider the cost of the program and if it is within your reach. Will you be able to work part- or full-time while studying, or will the program require all your time and attention? The answer to this question will determine how you budget for tuition costs and living expenses. Finally, consider what you will be taking away from any program: will you have a meaningful and valuable certificate from a recognized and reputable culinary institution? Does the program offer professional connections and employment assistance or job placement after graduation? Will it give you the opportunity to intern or work in restaurants while in school? Don't be afraid to ask a lot of questions when you go to visit schools. If you can't visit all the schools you're interested in, make sure to contact an admissions officer or academic adviser with any questions you have.

chapter 4

WORKING FOR YOUR DAILY BREAD

C ulinary school is one option for obtaining a thorough knowledge of the culinary world. Even if you do go to culinary school, however, you cannot graduate and immediately become the head chef of your own restaurant. Every chef starts at (or near) the bottom and works his or her way up through patience, perseverance, and practice. Ever wondered what Emeril Lagasse's first job in the food industry was? Emeril—who is now the author of several books, owns multiple restaurants, and has a long-running cooking show—started out washing pots and pans in a bakery. Dieter Schorner, who was named one of the top pastry chefs in the world by *Time* magazine, started out salting pretzels. And Judy Rodgers, who has published cookbooks from her acclaimed San Fransisco restaurant, the Zuni Cafe, started out working in a Dairy Queen.

Clearly, there's no shame in paying your dues in the culinary world. The only way to grow and learn as a chef is to start small, get your foot in a kitchen door, and work as hard as you can. First jobs are an important learning experience. One of the first things that every chef must learn is to be humble and to bring the same enthusiasm and attention to detail to any task, no matter how small or basic. From making sure each pretzel is expertly salted to mopping the floors of a fast food restaurant,

Before chef Emeril Lagasse was adding his signature "Bam!" to the culinary world, he was just a teenager working his first job in a Portuguese bakery in a small town in Massachusetts.

no chef should consider any job beneath him or her. Each job should be treated as a learning experience that will ultimately create a better, more well-rounded, and more talented and experienced chef.

One of the reasons that even culinary school graduates must apprentice and practice their craft is that it's hard to understand what work is like in a professional kitchen until you've experienced it firsthand.

INTERNSHIPS, APPRENTICESHIPS, AND YOUR FIRST JOB

Although some chefs will begin by trying to find a paying job—any job—in the culinary industry, there are a number of options for internships and apprenticeships in the industry. Before cooking schools became a common training ground for new chefs, many contemporary American chefs started out working as apprentices in restaurants all over the United States.

An apprenticeship means not just learning by observing, but being taught and mentored by a master in the industry. Some of these opportunities offer credentials just like culinary school programs. This means that, even for those chefs who opted to forgo culinary school, they will have official certification of the acquisition of required skills

Apprenticing is an option for culinary training if you can find a good mentor you would like to work with. More experienced chefs can offer valuable instruction and advice to young trainees.

and experience that they can put on their résumés when they look for jobs. The reasons for choosing to apprentice rather than attend culinary school can vary. The investment of time and money might keep some chefs out of the classroom, while others might find learning through hands-on, real-world professional experience to be a better fit for them.

Apprenticeship has its roots in European tradition. French chefs, some as young as thirteen years old, would learn the ways of cooking from master chefs. This system has remained largely unchanged in Europe, but the American apprenticeship system is less developed. There are fewer restaurants in the United States that are willing to take on novice chefs and train them, and laws in this country restrict the age of apprentices and limit how much they can work without pay. However, there is an exception to be found at the American Culinary Federation (ACF), which runs a three-year national apprenticeship training program for culinary students in the United States.

For those who don't want or are unable to land a coveted apprenticeship, the best way to really kick-start a culinary career is to land your first job. There's no substitute for the kind of hands-on education and experience you can get only in a kitchen. As you begin to look for a job, there are a number of things to consider. First of all, where would you like to work? Small town restaurants often have trouble finding good help, so there may be less competition for these positions. That said, the greatest concentration of restaurants, and particularly critically acclaimed restaurants, is usually in urban areas. If you do land a job at a top restaurant, don't expect a top-dollar salary to go with it. Because training under renowned chefs is considered a valuable learning experience, and because competition for these positions is so high, there is actually a good chance that the pay level is inversely proportional to the status of the restaurant.

THE EARLY CAREER OF MASTER CHEF ALLEN SUSSER

Allen Susser is a well-known chef who has won both the James Beard Foundation's Best Chef Award (one of the highest honors in cooking) and an honorary degree from Johnson & Wales University. He was named one of south Florida's hottest chefs for his unique culinary combinations and use of Florida's delicious natural resources in his restaurant.

However, before he was winning awards, Susser was just a boy from Brooklyn, New York, who wanted to learn to be a chef. In 1976, he graduated at the top of his class from the New York City Technical College Restaurant Management School. After graduating from culinary school, he pursued classical cooking techniques. Susser was determined to continue his studies by working in one of the top restaurants in New York City: Le Cirque. He ended up landing a job there but was making only $5 an hour—much less than he had been making at previous jobs.

Susser decided it was more important to be around the type of restaurant, food, and chefs that most interested him than to be paid well while learning his craft. Susser has said, "I thought that even after four years of school, it was more important to still learn rather than to look for dollars." Susser has experienced great success in his culinary career through abundant talent, creativity, passion, and hard work. He cautions aspiring chefs to think a great deal about their first restaurant jobs and how they will shape their ongoing education and future careers.

You also might have a preference for the size of the restaurant in which you would like to work. A larger restaurant will have a larger staff and turn out a high number of dishes each night. However, a smaller restaurant, one with fewer chefs in the kitchen, may give you the opportunity of taking on greater and more varied responsibilities because there are so few "hands on deck." Working at a hotel can also provide a wide variety of restaurant and kitchen experiences. No matter where your first job is, however, you will learn a lot.

Given so many options, it can be difficult to choose where you want to work. A good rule of thumb is to simply look for jobs at the places that interest you most. If you want to be a pastry chef, you should look for jobs in pastry shops or restaurants where you could work under a strong pastry chef. If you want to work in a restaurant, you should look for the type of restaurant where you feel most comfortable and whose menu and cooking styles you most admire. Set your sights on a kitchen where you can get the best possible learning experience. Much like picking a culinary school, choosing a place to learn or continue learning will benefit your overall culinary education, even if it is not the most high-paying position.

GETTING YOUR FOOT IN THE KITCHEN DOOR

So how do you go about landing your first job? As with any job, the first step is to write your résumé. It's important to emphasize all academic, volunteer, internship, and work experience that could be applicable and demonstrate your love of and passion for food. This is especially true if you are a new chef who might not have a long list of direct restaurant experience to put down. Consider any experience that might be applicable. If you worked at a farmers' market selling produce or even on a farm, you can use this experience to demonstrate your familiarity with the

If you're truly passionate about food, look for any job or position that will beef up your culinary résumé. This doesn't just include restaurants. Even working at a farmers' market can give you valuable knowledge of fresh ingredients and how the supply side of restaurants works.

farm-to-table ethic of modern cuisine. If you were a waiter or dishwasher in a restaurant previously, this can demonstrate your knowledge of how a kitchen works and your familiarity with restaurant hours. Even if you worked as a teller in a bank, the useful math skills you acquired might be relevant if you are an aspiring pastry chef who deals with math and measurements on a daily basis. These skills could also come in handy if you work in a smaller restaurant where you may be able to share responsibility for inventory management and balancing the books. Just remember, the most important thing about your résumé is that it conveys who you are, why you are passionate about food, and why you would be a good asset to any restaurant.

Make sure you do a lot of research on the restaurants to which you are applying. Study and memorize the menus, learn about the head chef, and read reviews. This is important both so that you will know if you want to apply there and also so that you can answer questions about why you want to work there if you get an interview. The people interviewing you will want to know why you chose their restaurant and what you are hoping to bring to the restaurant, as well as what you are hoping to take away from the experience. Successful chefs say that putting your résumé out there and waiting for interviews and job offers is an exercise in patience and persistence. It can take a long time and require a lot of legwork. The important thing is to not give up and to not take no for an answer.

If you are able to get an interview, be prepared to answer a lot of questions about your interest in food and what inspires you. You might be asked where you've traveled and what flavors are your favorite. The interviewer will also likely be interested in your goals and where you would like to be in a few years. The point of the interview is both to see if you are a good fit for the restaurant and to see if the restaurant is a good fit for you. In the interview, as in the résumé, the best thing you can do is convey your passion for food and cooking. Don't worry as

much about technical questions or knowing every possible cooking technique. Restaurants hiring new chefs are more concerned that you have the essential qualities and makings of a good chef, not necessarily every last skill. If you have the desire,

It isn't possible to learn every skill you will need on the job before you start. Every kitchen is different, and if you're willing to work hard and learn quickly most restaurants will be happy to help you through the learning curve.

will, passion, creativity, and basic talent required to be a chef, they will often be willing to train you on the job.

Some restaurants ask applicants to "trail" in the restaurant before signing them on to work full-time. Trailing really just

A successful chef maintains a clean, orderly workstation and does her best to stay organized even when things get hectic in the kitchen.

means working for free at the restaurant so the chefs can see how well you mesh with the rest of the team and with the restaurant as a whole. Because line chefs must work together like a well-oiled machine to get everything done, it is very important that each new chef who is hired works well with the other chefs. Unpaid trailing might sound like a raw deal, but it's actually a great opportunity for the applicant. While the restaurant is determining if the chef is right for it, the chef can also use this time to determine if the restaurant is the right choice for him or her. This gives the potential chef a chance to see how the kitchen operates and if he or she would prefer to work in a larger or smaller restaurant or one that serves a different style of food.

DEVELOPING GOOD WORK HABITS IN THE KITCHEN

Whether you are trailing, apprenticing, or working your first job, it is important to make a good impression. You want to arrive on time, if not early, for your shift every day. If you're not on time, you will look disorganized, which is one thing no chef can afford to be. When you have available time, you should also volunteer for any shifts that need filling, especially the weekend and holiday ones. It is important to make the best of on-the-job learning. Find a mentor who will help guide you and give you feedback. Feedback early in your career—both positive and negative—is important to any chef's growth and maturation as a culinary professional.

Equally important is learning to establish a daily plan that you can execute the same way every day. Take notes on each step that you are responsible for and make sure you keep your quality consistent no matter what step in the process you are handling. A good chef will always keep thorough notes, with a prep list and a diagram of what his or her workstation will look like. You might think you can remember everything and not write things down, but keep in mind that the prep list and station diagram will be changing as the menu changes, so keeping notes is a good way to not get confused or miss something.

You must master any task that is given to you. Developing good work habits and discipline early is the best thing you can do for yourself as a young chef. This way as you develop more skills and take on more responsibility, you have a good foundation to fall back on. From an unpaid kitchen hand chopping potatoes to the head chef of a large, popular restaurant, every chef needs the same basic skills and the same qualities to succeed.

chapter 5

THE FUTURE OF CULINARY ARTS

The culinary world is one that is constantly changing in response to what people are looking for when they go out to eat. A successful chef has to be aware of these trends and be prepared to offer the foods that people are hungry for. It is important for a chef to be able to adapt to these changes or risk getting left behind.

EATING GREEN: CULINARY TRENDS TO WATCH

In recent years, one of the biggest culinary trends has been that people have started caring not just about how their food tastes but where it comes from. There is an increasing interest in eating organic foods and those that are locally grown. People are also more interested in eating healthier. They are often willing to pay more for better ingredients. A 2011 survey by the National Restaurant Association found that 71 percent of adults say that they try to eat healthier now at restaurants than they did two years ago. Additionally, a whopping 69 percent of adults say that they are more likely to visit a restaurant that offers food grown or raised in an organic or environmentally friendly way.

One way the food industry has responded to changing consumer interests is by creating new restaurants specializing in

As part of the culinary trend of cooking with organic, locally grown ingredients, some restaurants even have their own gardens so chefs can harvest the freshest produce right before cooking.

organic and locally sourced cuisine. Some chefs even form partnerships with local farmers or routinely shop for their ingredients at farmers' markets. People enjoy knowing that by eating at a certain restaurant they will be supporting the local farmers in their community. They will also know that by eating there, the food is very fresh because it will not have had to travel very far.

In addition to locally sourced and organic foods, there is also an emerging culinary trend toward sustainable seafood. Seafood that is sustainable includes those species of fish, shellfish, and mollusks that are not overharvested. There must be an abundance left in the ocean so that the species is not threatened by large-scale commercial fishing and harvesting. Additionally, fish that are farmed in ways that negatively impact the environment are not considered sustainable.

There is also a rapidly growing interest in gluten-free menu items for gluten-sensitive and gluten-intolerant restaurant-goers. Adding a few gluten-free items to a menu can give a restaurant an edge over its competition as more and more people follow a gluten-free or gluten-reduced diet.

SMALL PLATES AND BIG SCIENCE

In addition to growing consumer interest in healthier eating and fresh, locally sourced, organic, and ethically grown or harvested foods, another culinary trend is for small plates. This doesn't just mean food that is served on saucers. These small plates are essentially appetizer-sized portions from which you can make a meal. The idea of small plates crosses all types of cuisine, from Spanish tapas to Chinese dim sum. It is becoming increasingly popular among diners as these scaled-down portions are being dished out more and more around the country.

The small plates concept works well for customers because they are no longer forced to choose just one entree—they can

BLUE HILL AT STONE BARNS

A number of restaurants have embraced the farm-to-table movement, in which the menus are composed of locally farmed, organic, seasonal ingredients. Blue Hill at Stone Barns in New York is a restaurant that takes farm-to-table a step farther—it brings the tables to the farm itself. Stone Barns Center for Food and Agriculture, where the Blue Hill restaurant is located, is a working four-season farm that produces quality ingredients.

Blue Hill at Stone Barns is different from any other restaurant experience. Instead of being greeted by a menu in the traditional sense when you reach your table, you are instead given a list of ingredients. You can request the number of courses and specify certain ingredients that you would not like used in your meal, but after that you leave the fate of your dinner up to the chef. Luckily, you and your meal are both in very good hands.

The chef who owns Blue Hill is Dan Barber. Barber has been named one of the Best New Chefs by *Food and Wine* magazine as well as a Top Chef in America by the James Beard Foundation. He is a big proponent of the local and sustainable food movement. The idea behind Barber's food is to make something delicious using seasonal foods organically grown right outside his kitchen door.

First Lady Michelle Obama, a strong advocate for healthy eating, stands with executive chef Dan Barber of Blue Hill at Stone Barns as they teach local children about the importance of fresh ingredients.

try a number of different things on the menu. It also has the added benefit of being very social, since small plates are often meant to be shared. While the model is customer friendly, it also works well for restaurants because, while each plate has

The culinary trend of small plates, such as Chinese dim sum (seen here) is popular with diners because they can try small amounts of many delicious things.

smaller quantities of food and is often cheaper than an entree, diners will often order several of them. Additionally, food can be served as soon as it is prepared. Serving a table of six people who have ordered traditionally sized entrees requires split-second

timing and careful communication in the kitchen so that all six entrees are ready to go to the table at the same time. However, with small plates that will be shared by all the guests at the table, food can go out piping hot as soon as it's ready, requiring far less of a juggling act.

Another trend in recent years has been a focus on high-tech cooking. Beyond the grill or oven, there are a number of advanced cooking techniques that chefs have only begun to explore. For example, chefs have been known to use molecular additives like liquid nitrogen to give their food a certain effect. Another cooking method that has taken off in recent years is the sous vide method. *Sous vide* means "under vacuum." Using this method, food is cooked by sealing it in airtight plastic packages and submerging it in warm water for long periods of time. The

Executive chef Pino Maffeo at Restaurant L, in Boston, Massachusetts, uses liquid nitrogen and a centrifuge to add flavor and complexity to his culinary creations.

intention is to cook the item evenly and avoid overcooking the outside, while still keeping the inside at the same level of "doneness." This makes it easier to keep the food tender and juicy but still fully cooked.

THE CULINARY INDUSTRY AND THE ECONOMY

As an aspiring chef, it is important to see why this career has become such an essential part of the economy. It is not only that the job of creating and serving food is an essential part of life and central to the modern North American lifestyle. The culinary industry itself makes up a huge part of the economy. It is an industry that is continuously growing and expanding, as more and more people enjoy going out to eat or ordering takeout from a favorite neighborhood restaurant as opposed to going to the store, buying food, cooking, and cleaning up. In the 1950s, the restaurant industry accounted for only a quarter of the total dollars Americans spent on food. Today, money spent in restaurants accounts for nearly half of all money spent on food.

Restaurant industry sales are around $600 billion a year, and restaurants employ around thirteen million people. Chefs, waiters, dishwashers, managers, and everyone else who makes a restaurant function account for around 10 percent of the United States workforce. So you see, restaurants are not just important for people to celebrate a special occasion, share leisure time with friends, or enjoy a delicious meal they didn't have to shop for, cook, or clean up after; restaurants are also an essential part of the economy itself.

The restaurant industry is a huge part of the United States economy. One out of every ten American workers is employed by the food service industry in some capacity.

While not all chef and food preparation jobs are recession-proof, there is a great deal of growth in the restaurant industry. The U.S. Bureau of Labor Statistics projects that there will be around 350,000 new jobs created for chefs, cooks, and food preparation workers by the year 2016.

If you have the drive and passion for food and the willingness to put in a lot of hard work, it is quite possible for you to be one of these new workers. You might not become a celebrity chef or be featured on television. But if you love food, cooking, and making people happy with your culinary creations, this could be the ideal career for you to earn money while doing something for which you have a passion. Choosing to become a chef means choosing long hours and few weekends or holidays off, but for someone who has a passion for food, it can be an ideal path to a rewarding career. And chefs are one essential career that is here to stay.

glossary

ambience The mood or atmosphere created by an environment.

apprenticeship The system in which a person learns a craft through mentoring by a master of that craft.

chain restaurant A restaurant that has a number of different locations and is owned or overseen by a parent company.

chef de partie A chef who is in charge of a particular station in a kitchen. Sometimes known as a station cook or line cook.

commis An assistant to a chef; usually considered a training position.

culinary Of or relating to cooking.

executive chef The chef who has the top authority in the kitchen, sometimes known as the head chef.

expediting Helping to pace cooking so that dishes all leave the kitchen at the right time.

externship Working in a restaurant, either paid or unpaid, as a learning experience. Similar to an internship but often shorter in duration.

franchise A business that the owner is allowed to run under the auspices and oversight of a larger corporation.

garde-manger A chef who manages cold items, such as salads or cold appetizers.

knife skills Part of a chef's skill set, dealing with different techniques for cutting and chopping.

line cook A chef who is in charge of a particular station in a kitchen. Sometimes known as a station cook or chef de partie.

local Food that is grown or produced close to where it is consumed.

organic Food that is grown in an environment free of pesticides and chemicals.

prep cook A chef who helps ready ingredients for other chefs to cook.

sous-chef The second-in-command in a kitchen under the head chef.

station cook A chef who is assigned to work at a specific station within a kitchen. Sometimes known as a line cook or chef de partie.

sustainable Food that is grown, raised, or harvested with minimal impact on the environment.

toque A tall white hat, traditionally worn by chefs.

trailing Working in a restaurant on a trial basis, usually without being paid.

for more information

American Culinary Federation (ACF)
180 Center Place Way
St. Augustine, FL 32095
(904) 824-4468
Web site: http://www.acfchefs.org
The ACF is a professional organization for chefs and cooks
that was founded in 1929. It offers seminars and work-
shops on the latest in industry trends, career recognition,
and accreditation for culinary education.

Canadian Culinary Federation
P.O. Box 3156
Courtenay, BC V9N 5N4
Canada
(250) 338-2720
Web site: http://www.ccfcc.ca
The Canadian Culinary Federation is a nonprofit organization
founded in 1963 to unite Canada's chefs and culinary
professionals. Membership is available to any and all persons
who actively seek career paths as a chef or chef-in-training.
They offer job assistance, training, and industry news.

Culinary Institute of America (CIA)
1946 Campus Drive
Hyde Park, NY 12538-1499
(845) 452-9600
Web site: http://www.ciachef.edu
The CIA is a private, not-for-profit college dedicated to
providing professional culinary education. Founded in
1946, it is the oldest culinary school in the United States.

Culinary Institute of Canada at Holland College
4 Sydney Street
Charlottetown, PEI C1A 1E9
Canada
(902) 894-6868
Web site: http://www.hollandcollege.com/
    culinary_institute_of_canada
The Culinary Institute of Canada, located at Holland
    College's Tourism and Culinary Centre, has provided
    culinary and hotel and restaurant management training
    since 1983. It offers degrees in culinary arts, pastry arts,
    culinary operations, and hotel and restaurant
    management.

Institute of Culinary Education (ICE)
50 West 23rd Street, # 5
New York, NY 10010
(212) 847-0700
Web site: http://www.iceculinary.com
The ICE is the largest and most active center for culinary
    education in New York City. It was founded in 1975 by
    Peter Kump and offers well-respected eight- to thirteen-
    month career training programs in culinary arts, pastry
    and baking, culinary management, and hospitality
    management.

James Beard Foundation
167 West 12th Street
New York, NY 10011
(212) 627-1111
Web site: http://www.jamesbeard.org
The James Beard Foundation is a New York City–based
    nonprofit dedicated to exploring the way food enriches
    people's lives. It is best known for the awards it gives out

to culinary professionals at the top of their field in all aspects of the industry—from chefs and restaurateurs to cookbook authors, food journalists, and restaurant designers and architects.

WEB SITES

Due to the changing nature of Internet links, Rosen Publishing has developed an online list of Web sites related to the subject of this book. This site is updated regularly. Please use this link to access this list:

http://www.rosenlinks.com/ECAR/Chef

for further reading

Achatz, Grant, and Nick Kokonas. *Life on the Line: A Chef's Story of Chasing Greatness, Facing Death, and Redefining the Way We Eat.* New York, NY: Gotham, 2012.

Adato, Allison. *Smart Chefs Stay Slim: Lessons in Eating and Living from America's Best Chefs.* New York, NY: New American Library, 2012.

Bourdain, Anthony. *Medium Raw: A Bloody Valentine to the World of Food and the People Who Cook.* New York, NY: Ecco, 2011.

Chalmers, Irena. *Food Jobs: 150 Great Jobs for Culinary Students, Career Changes, and Food Lovers.* New York, NY: Beaufort Books, 2008.

Culinary Institute of America. *The Professional Chef.* Hoboken, NJ: Wiley, 2011.

Dixon, Jonathan. *Beaten, Seared, and Sauced: On Becoming a Chef at the Culinary Institute of America.* New York, NY: Clarkson Potter, 2011.

Ferriss, Timothy. *The 4-Hour Chef: The Simple Path to Cooking Like a Pro, Learning Anything, and Living the Good Life.* New York, NY: Houghton Mifflin Harcourt, 2012.

Gold, Rozanne. *Eat Fresh Food: Awesome Recipes for Teen Chefs.* New York, NY: Bloomsbury USA Children's, 2009.

Hamilton, Dorothy, and Patric Kuh. *Chef's Story: 27 Chefs Talk About What Got Them into the Kitchen.* New York, NY: Harper Perennial, 2008.

Hamilton, Gabrielle. *Blood, Bones, & Butter: The Inadvertent Education of a Reluctant Chef.* New York, NY: Random House, 2012.

Hill, Kathleen Thompson. *Career Opportunities in the Food and Beverage Industry.* Cuddy, PA: Ferguson Publishing, 2010.

Lankford, Ronnie D. *Is Organic Food Better?* Farmington Hills, MI: Greenhaven Press, 2011.

Page, Karen, and Andrew Dorenburg. *The Flavor Bible: The Essential Guide to Culinary Creativity, Based on the Most Imaginative Chef's in America.* New York, NY: Little, Brown, 2008.

Potter, Jeff. *Cooking for Geeks: Real Science, Great Hacks, and Good Food.* Sebastopol, CA: O'Reilly Media, 2010.

Ruhlman, Michael. *The Making of a Chef: Mastering Heat at the Culinary Institute of America.* New York, NY: Holt Paperbacks, 2009.

Senker, Cath. *Hospitality and Catering Careers.* Mankato, MN: Amicus, 2010.

Shulman, Margaret Rose. *Culinary Boot Camp: Five Days of Basic Training at the Culinary Institute of America.* New York, NY: Wiley, 2006.

Weinstein, Norma, and Mark Thomas. *Mastering Knife Skills: The Essential Guide to the Most Important Tools in Your Kitchen.* New York, NY: Stewart, Tabori & Chang, 2008.

bibliography

AiInSite. "Culinary and Food Trends for 2012." January 30, 2012. Retrieved February 2012 (http://insite.artinstitutes. edu/culinary-and-food-trends-for-2012-69362. aspx?source=AINST).

American Culinary Federation. "About ACF." Retrieved October 2011 (http://www.acfchefs.org).

Chalmers, Irena. *Food Jobs: 150 Great Jobs for Culinary Students, Career Changes, and Food Lovers*. New York, NY: Beaufort Books, 2008.

Cohen, Jeff. *The Complete Idiot's Guide to Recession-Proof Careers*. New York, NY: Penguin Group, 2010.

Culinary Institute of America. "About the Culinary Institute of America." Retrieved February 2012 (http://www.ciachef.edu).

Dixon, Jonathan. *Beaten, Seared, and Sauced: On Becoming a Chef at the Culinary Institute of America*. New York, NY: Clarkson Potter, 2011.

Dorenburg, Andrew, and Karen Page. *Becoming a Chef: Revised Edition*. New York, NY: John Wiley & Sons, 2003.

Institute of Culinary Education. "Culinary School Career Training: Program Overview." Retrieved February 2012 (http://www.iceculinary.com/career/index.shtml).

Johnson & Wales University. "College of Culinary Arts." Retrieved February 2012 (http://www.jwu.edu/culinary).

Levine, Ed. "Blue Hill at Stone Barns: The Most Important Restaurant in America." Serious Eats, June 17, 2008. Retrieved February 2012 (http://newyork.seriouseats. com/2008/06/blue-hill-at-stone-barns-pocantico-hills-new-york-dan-barber- working-farm.html).

MilitaryChefs.com. "Certifications." Retrieved February 2012 (http://www.militarychefs.com).

National Restaurant Association. "2012 Restaurant Industry Forecast: Facts at a Glance." Retrieved February 2012 (http://restaurant.org/research/facts).

Ruhlman, Michael. *The Making of a Chef: Mastering Heat at the Culinary Institute of America*. New York, NY: Holt Paperbacks, 2009.

Yuko Kitazawa. *Career Diary of a Pastry Chef* (Gardner's Guide Series). Chicago, IL: Garth Gardner Company, 2008.

index

ABOUT THE AUTHOR

Susan Meyer is a writer living and working in New York City—
one of the greatest food cities in the world. Meyer is an amateur
chef operating within the severe limitations of her apartment's
small kitchen, but leaves the serious culinary creations up to
the professionals. Her culinary tour of New York State has
taken her to one of the restaurants at the Culinary Institute of
America, and she hopes to visit Blue Hill at Stone Barns soon.

PHOTO CREDITS

Cover © iStockphoto.com/Denis Raev; cover (background), p. 1
Ronald Sumners/Shutterstock.com; back cover © iStockphoto
.com/blackred; p. 4 michaeljung/Shutterstock.com; pp. 6–7 Life
Productions/Thinkstock; pp. 10–11 Jupiterimages/Comstock/
Thinkstock; pp. 12–13 Gerry Penny/AFP/Getty Images; pp. 15,
26–27 Jetta Productions/Iconica/Getty Images; pp. 16–17, 54
Jupiterimages/Goodshoot/Thinkstock; pp. 22, 38–39 © AP
Images; p. 24 Otna Ydur/Shutterstock.com; p. 30 Thomas
Northcut/Digital Vision/Thinkstock; pp. 34–35 Fuse/Getty
Images; pp. 36–37 Jonathan Feinstein/Shutterstock.com; p. 41
U.S. Navy photo by Mass Communication Specialist Joseph M.
Buliavac; pp. 44–45 Pam Francis/Getty Images; p. 46 Monkey
Business Images/Shutterstock.com; p. 50 Valerie E. Steffl; pp.
52–53 Moritz Hoffmann/LOOK/Getty Images; p. 58 Stefano
Scata/FoodPix/Getty Images; pp. 60–61 Peter Foley/EPA/Landov;
pp. 62–63 Hywit Dimyadi/Shutterstock.com; pp. 64–65 Brian
Snyder/Reuters/Landov; pp. 66–67 Allison Dinner/StockFood
Creative/Getty Images.

Designer: Matt Cauli; Photo Researcher: Karen Huang

641.
5
M

Meyer, Susan.

A career as a chef